less is more, more or less

< o >

MEZCALITA PRESS, LLC
Norman, OK

Cover Design: Chris Everett
Cover Photos: iStock by Getty Images™

MEZCALITA PRESS, LLC
Norman, Oklahoma

Also by Nathan Brown:

You don't need many words if you
already know what you're talking about,

~ William Stafford
"By a River in the Osage Country"

less is more,
more or less

< O >

~ Nathan Brown ~

table of contents

Acknowledgements

Certain poems more or less appeared in:

Malpaís Review – "Perpetual" and "Testament"
Red River Review – "Baylor," "Complicated,"
"Condolence," "Editor," "Eulogy for a Bastard,"
and "Recovering"
Walt's Corner in the *Long-Islander* newspaper –
"Presbyopia"

Many thanks to those publications.

More thanks to the Oklahoma Humanities
Council for all their support and guidance.

Even more thanks to Chris Everett for the
magical graphic design he brings to the table.

And no less thanks to Mom and Dad, who have
sacrificed so much over the years, this book
should be considered a co-write.

Sierra. Always.

The slightly more than short quotation from
Stephen King, in the poem "Write," is in his
book: *On Writing: A Memoir of the Craft.*

More and more…

for
Ashley

less is more,
more or less

< o >

LESS THAN LESS

More is
filled with extras
and aches to have them all.
Since having the most is
the reason for the game.

Which in the stretch
becomes problematic
because of the inevitable
way that "moreness"
negates the possibility
of "enoughness"

and therefore
creates a certain
"neverness"
that kills
all joy.

but enough
about me

< O >

*I think Narcissism is the system
that means the most to me.*

~ Tony Hoagland

STRAIN

Part Cherokee
and part English.

With all of the genes
and inky stains of Irish
and a well-aged Scotch.

Enough ancestral shades
to wash and fade into
the colorlessness
of irrelevance.

NOTHING

Some day
some young person
may see me take a stand
and think, *O how brave…*
      What a brave old man.

And some other old man
may not bother to tell her,
No, my dear… He is just tired,
with nothing left to lose. That's all.

And he may not bother to tell
because he is tired as well,
with nothing really
to gain.

CONDOLENCE

I turn 48 this day.
So, 49 in 365 more.
And yes… you know
you're starting to look it
when the birthday jokes
of your better friends
sound softer this year.

Maybe one of them
lets a heavy-hitter slip
while averting his gaze
to the whole-grain cake
with only a few candles.
Because of the fire code.

But mostly though,
they are all   so   sorry
this is happening to you.

HERMIT

There is always some
jackhammer pounding
down on the corner
of Paradise and Main

    with maybe a band saw
    somewhere behind it
        off in some
        not quite enough
        amount of distance.

It makes me crave
a sort of shanty isolation,
a wood-burning desolation,
out in the frozen elsewheres
of the much less desirable.

KNEE

What the tender earth giveth

the concrete sidewalk
taketh away

in the cartilage
between thy femur
and thy patella.

PRESBYOPIA

Words on the page
now require an extra
foot or so from my eyes
for me to find them.

Just the latest
in a long line of lovers
to politely and apologetically
distance herself from me.

FAITH

The size of a mustard seed.

That's all it takes, Jesus said.
All you need, said Mrs. Morton,
a 4th grade Sunday School teacher.

And after all these errant years,
several lost decades-worth,
I still stare at mountains...

   waiting, half-crazed...

for any sign of movement.

UNIVERSITY

I spent 23 good years
and my parents' savings
deboning its favorite texts
for the title and deed
to the grave privilege
of calling a crock
a crock
when I see it
stewing and steaming
before me.

FAUX PAS

Sometimes my answers
to simple questions
unfurl like massive
and tragic oil spills,

engulfing light conversation
in sad, sickening slicks
of inky devastation,

impulsive spurts of social blunder
aggregating into bilious clouds
of impropriety and immeasurable
coast to coast destruction.

PSYCHOTHERAPY

                                        … for Dr. Z.

It is not as much
the *he*, but more
it, as a process,
that I distrust.

This digging way
down to bottoms,
places I'd vowed
never to return.

Places that
once there,
even he said,
Oh my God.

RACE

I took my turn.

Lived with the gas pedal
smashed to the floorboard.

My wheels going elliptical
with the best intentions
I could marshal.

At least until
I discovered
there is no
finish line.

TIRE

Too many
holes now.

I cannot
keep the air
from escaping.

BURNOUT

Those days come. Days
when the old dirty bulb
that swings in my brain
only flickers and buzzes.

I screw it tighter, tap it
with a calloused finger,
but get little to no light.

SURVIVALIST

As we begin our approach
to the next great World War,

    and the vexing separation
    of all national economies
    that it's bound to cause,

it worries me to all ends
that I will not be able
to grow coffee beans
in Central Texas.

SISSY

Woolen socks.
Big fluffy slippers.
Coffee n' a pancake.

A little music now
from the soundtrack
of *Breakfast at Tiffany's.*

A candle, and a knitted
afghan draped over thighs
and gathered around my feet
on a bright February barely
held at bay by the sunroom
behind my parents' house.

And as I bring French Roast
and fine China to my lips I think,

Hey man. It's cold.
                    Alright?

ELEVATOR

I love a backlit button
with a big "G" on it.

The "1" often lies.

And who knows where
the white glowing circle
with a black star on it
will take you? No.

As with altimeters,
so with elevators:

just tell me where
the ground is,
please.

RIDE

To move from Oklahoma
to Texas involves
a certain amount
of sinking,
a falling,

the stomach
rising into the throat
as all I've ever known
disappears behind
that last rise
in the tracks.

NEW

First night
in the new house.
New town. New state.

The last time I did this
was the first time I'd done it,
43 years ago, back when I came
from the state I've come to now.

And I don't recall it being so hard
to become a new citizen. But...
I wasn't quite five-years-old
the first time I did this,
and mom and dad
were in charge.

TRAVELER

I leave
more places
than I arrive to,
in the end.

And I wonder
where that puts me
on the map.

PERPETUAL

On many days
here in Santa Fe,
I walk up Canyon Road
and back down Palace
to the plaza—as if
toward some promise.

Or, is it away from
all those broken.

But mostly
in circles.

Donkey Hoty

We lived only once.

~ Adam Zagajewski

Too many years
carrying and listening to
this Sancho on my shoulder

to try and get
the Quixote
off my back.

OF RICHES

What my parents
have done without

would shock the average
American shopping mall.

What they possess though,
should shame, if not mortify,

the three hundred or so members
of the Augusta National Golf Club.

GOOGOL:

the number of times
my daughter has typed
the letters *o m* and *g*
      or *l o* and *l*
into her smartphone

multiplied by

the number of times
I've sat and stared
at my dumb one
wishing she
would call

Teenager

She wants me to stay close,
but not to hang around—

> a backup gun, loaded
> with bullets of short
> sweet text messages,
> some gas money, and
> occasional praise for
> her accomplishments,

> that she secretly keeps
> in her backpack or on
> her bedside table when
> she tries to sleep at night.

WITHHELD

A thousand and three
   little truths hanging
      in an untold limbo.

Their forever silence
   forever ringing
      in a daughter's
         precious ears.

TOO EARLY

It's too late to say
　　It's too early.

She is driving now,
for less than a year,
and has just released
a six song EP on iTunes
and Amazon required
to carry the label:

> **PARENTAL**
> **ADVISORY**
> EXPLICIT LYRICS

TOO LATE

It's too early to say
 It's too late,

when the atoms
of a parent's love
still fly in great circles,
colliding at speeds enough
to power a fledgling sun...

and the prayers of prophets
and grandmothers still burn
with enough ionic passion
to revive a fibrillated God.

THE QUESTION

I remember it well.

And the way it loomed
as some dark guarantee
over the lowered brow
of every father of every
girl   I   ever   dated:

> *Well, yeah…*
>
> > *but what*
> > *do you* really *do?*

WIFE

She is, in the end,
my better three-fourths.

Let's face it.
I bring at most
a fourth of anything
worth putting under a microscope
to this budding matrimony.

And if you're thinking,

*Really? I'd say
a sixteenth at best.*

I won't fight you on it.

GOODWIFE

She pulled my heart
up from the floor,

leaned its back
against the wall
next to the couch,

and brought bowls
of hot soup and cups
of fresh coffee until
the feeling began
to return.

DIAMOND APOLOGY

It is the day before
our second anniversary,
and I owe my wife an apology.

And I don't mean one of those
knock-off, under-the-counter-
at-Walmart, or-even-Dillard's,
piece-o'-crap-Zirconium things.

I mean something with a real
shine of humility to it. The cut
of an almost crystalline sincerity
that proves my wholehearted
and, I'd go as far as to say,
absolutely igneous
sorriness.

ANNIVERSARY

In a hundred years,
if the earth spins on
past the limits
of my breath,

these pages
will continue
to pulse and sing
along the banks
of my love
for you.

BLUSH

The soft lines
and sculpted edges
of her profound beauty
remain hidden, veiled
to her own eyes…

which makes them burn
all the more before mine
with the light and heat
of a thousand candles.

SLOWPOKE

I am falling
in love.

Have been
for almost
seven years now.

I like to take my time
when it comes to
the bigger
things.

CLEAR

Worry does not empty tomorrow of its
sorrow, it empties today of its strength.

~ Corrie ten Boom

She cut little sayings
by Corrie ten Boom
and Thich Nhat Nanh
out of an Oprah magazine
to tape onto walls and mirrors.

Sayings on what worry does not
accomplish and how beautiful
this moment is. Sayings taped,
I noticed, to the mirror above
my sink, the wall above my
writing table, making clear
who needs them most.

RECOVERING

Having grown up
a Southern Baptist,
I awake still, here
in my almost 50s,

with a sense of shock
and divine fear that
there is a sexy
    and naked
woman lying
next to me in bed.

    And that this
    is somehow
    okay with God.

SELF-IMPOSED

I should.
    I know.
For the sake of
others, and myself.

Live in a scorpion-infested
bamboo hut among the jaguar
in the dark jungles of Belize.

Alone.

But I love my wife
    so much.
And I want her
    to keep me.

But Enough about Me

The one who viewed
my poems as a hobby
at best—sized them up
as a passing phase, if not
an embarrassment of sorts—
was baffled when I left her.

But she was utterly incensed
when I later married a woman
who loves them. Well, except
for maybe the ones about
the women in my past.

a parliament
of owls

< O >

Well, go ahead and call the cops
You don't meet nice girls in coffee shops

~ Tom Waits

COFFEE

Electrochemical
pulses of caffeination
lurk and loll in the tide
of my plasma sea,

little dorsal fins
of joy and the jolt
of frisky endorphins
that bob and glide along
the glinting shoreline
of my sacred
and unseen
waters.

TOOL

I heard
this morning,
    somewhere
    out my window,

    a meticulous raven
tapping out his memoir
on a fence pipe
with a nail.

I'M ONE TO TALK

The walls
are painted orange
in The Red Cup.

And there are other things
I love about it as well.

Like the gaggle of regulars
who appear to get by
without working.

EXORCISE

She likes a Pilates Ball
and power-walking
with hand weights.

But the Zumba craze
is over now and, besides,

the new yoga instructor
at the downtown studio
is hot and doing wonders
for her raging sciatica
and sex dreams. Anything

to help her work it out
of her circuit-fried system.

CONTRITION

To pay for his own,
he cuts and clears the way
for expensive new homes
out in the Texas hills.

And to his surprise,
he feels a little twinge,
    the tweak of it,
in his shoulders

every time
the grinding teeth
in the rotating chain
sink their sharp joy
into the skin of yet
another live oak.

COMPLICATED

She's headed out there
to the coast of sunsets
and evanescent stars

to hook up with a guy
that the ex-wife of
a guy she just dumped

set her up with in order
for them both to screw over
their three ex-husbands.

DRIP

The volume
and depth
came on
so slowly,

he never thought
to build a boat.

FISHWIFE

It was the smell
of the job, you know,
that gave her such
a foul mouth...

the relentless odor,
she could not wash out
of her apron and hair,
that she cursed.

LOCAL STAR

He's still
as good
as he ever
was.

That's why
he's still
where
he is.

Too

At seventeen,
she is bursting
at every seam,

> every joint
> and follicle,

with knowledge
she should not
> yet
> > possess.

Chameleonic

She is
a rainbow
of self-preservation.

Every tint
and shade
a postcard home

with little notes
and faded stamps
marking the margins
of all she has survived.

WIDE-EYED

Sometimes
with wonder
and amazement...

but more often
from the life
that somehow
got away from her.

And for the love of God
and all that is holy,
she can't figure out
where the hell it went.

Fix

WAKE THE DEAD
COFFEEHOUSE
Ranch Road 12
San Marcos, Texas

where the recently
undead gather 'round

with pale-veined hands
and gauzy red eyes

to sip a pleasant
witch's brew

and yet remain
relatively unawakened.

59

MUDSMITH

This is
Dallas.
And it is
in Texas.
And this is
a coffee shop
on Greenville.
And so there is
a 5–point buck's
head on the wall
just above my table
staring in disbelief
at the sad puniness
of all human craving
and gastronomical greed.

BAYLOR

Baptist college girls
in tight and tiny
blue jean shorts,

thighs beaming
on all frequencies,

garbling any and all
of God's broadcasts
on the wages of sin.

HIPPIES

The real ones have
lower-back pain now
and ponytails hanging
by only a few gray threads.

They've had to switch
to the Velcro sandals lately
because of rheumatoid arthritis.

And though they remember
some of the main principles
of The Sixties Revolution,

they've stopped for coffee
on the side-streets in Taos
and seem to be having a
helluva time getting up
from their seats.

HIPSTER

At the table next.
Huddled up n' filthy.
All thumbs on an iPhone.
Hat dirty because he doesn't
wash his hair. Black hair, greazy
because he doesn't wash the hat.

And we expect the odious ennui,
the matted beard—as well as
the secondhand knock-off
Navy pea coat with a film
of cat hair on the hem.

But dog shit too?

INTENSE

The spunky young activists
are all activating at the table
next to mine. All smartphones,
laptops, and vegetarian chili.

And I'm all coffee n' chocolate
and leather journal. Yanking
at the balls of the world
in my own quiet way.

CON-TORNFLICTED

She's not a regular
here at The Red Cup,
and yet still managed

to waltz around the corner
and snag my favorite table
before I could claim it.

And now,
she's parked there
all smug-snuggled up

with a Frito Chili Pie,
a glass of sweet iced tea,
and a shiny new edition of

my latest book.

INCOGNITO

I live,
all of a sudden,
in a small town in Texas
where no one knows me.

So I come to sit, alone,
in a corner by a window
of the only coffee shop

and root like a wild boar
in the beautiful mud
of anonymity.

    They do not know.
        They do not know.

REQUEST

To every musician
the request will come.
If not tonight, then
next week, or year.

And it will arrive
from the back row.
Sometimes the front.

Or maybe slip in at your feet,
handwritten in black Sharpie
on a white cocktail napkin.

As it did to me last night:

PLAY FREEBIRD

WASTELAND

A colossal sound system
on a massive black stage
with well-trained lasers.

A bright, mighty vessel
built especially to help
guitar-thrashing bands

of angst-beaten hipsters
deliver over everything
they do not have to say.

iLONE TOGETHER

The other night,
over a quiet dinner
at the Snack Bar
on South Congress,

my wife and I became
those people sucked into
the narcotic glow of iPhones.

Talking, not quite to each other.
Smiling, not quite at each other.

It lasted less than a minute.
But I'm still, days later,
sad about it.

NIRVANA

There are surely many
lotus-laden pathways
leading to perfect bliss
and the ultimate loss
of my individuality.

One that I know of
winds its way through
the Southwest where
the best bartenders
salt the wide rim,
then shake and pour
my mad margarita
without a word
between us.

EULOGY

In the dimly lit
sanctuary of a stool
down at the far end
of the Anasazi bar,

I sit and never quite
deliver a few final words
over the salt and melted ice
at the bottom of
the evening's
last margarita.

A PARLIAMENT OF OWLS

sits in the far corner
of The Red Cup,
blinking and twisting
their heads away from
a drove of asses braying
at the table next to them.

Like a culture of bacteria
we gather in this Petri dish
to sip in the dizzy shadows
of a business of flies buzzing
above an otherwise quiet
labor of moles.

ars poetica:

poems
and their problems

< O >

*Just because people don't understand you,
it doesn't mean you're a poet.*

~ Richard Ray

CODA

The saddest
little moment
in my sometimes
happy mornings

is always the moment
when I place the period
there at the very end
of the last little
sentence,

like this one.

SKYSCRAPER

... for Don Dorsey

Tired of being told
it was the limit,

he chiseled
through showers
of sparks, battled
with bombs of light,

and set big colorful fires
at its invisible boundaries,

determined to break through
the earth's imperious ceiling
so we could see further
than we ever have
before.

SEAFOOD

Church towers rest on the ocean's floor,

~ Adam Zagajewski

Such endeavor. All these
lines, and commas,
chiseled into verse.

So many trees
cut to print them
on human-made leaves.

Such woeful, crestfallen
little castles and kingdoms
made of words and cards.

All these lyrical spires
little more than fodder
for the rising of the seas.

MAGNA OPERA

From Puccini
   to Pablo Picasso,
      Basho to Beethoven,

civilization's sapient cloud
of witnesses and prophets
pulses with power to sing
beyond the Apocalypse,

as Sappho
   and Sharon Olds
      shock awake
         the very ear
           and heart

of dark matter itself.

DEMOGRAPHIC

I picture her with coffee,
    a fourth grade teacher
reading one of my poems
in the break room before
going back to her class.

I see him in an orange vest,
    one of my books open
in his left hand, a sign
in his right telling traffic
to SLOW down as the bandana
on his head whips in the gusts
of their inattention. Else,

I imagine no one at all.

READER

To you,
who made it this far
into a book of small poems,

I raise this morning's cup.

And now,
if you will raise yours as well—

A toast!

To the rarified
any and all
who have managed
to be both alive
and awake.

EDITOR

I submit to you
this poem that might,
I am afraid, make sense
to some of your readers.

And only because I thought
they might enjoy the break—
a snow day we could call it—

from the rather demanding
leaves of severe profundity
you normally supply us,

and that we do at least
understand are for
our own good.

VOICES

They have teeth,
worn and polished
from years of use.

A tongue just as lethal.

But your critics
would not
love you

if you
changed.

REMEMBER,

if you cut back on
animal fat and sugar,
ride bike regularly,
work hard every day
at improving your craft
and eventually receive
awards, prizes, and titles
recognizing your efforts,

many people, even some
who were once your friends,

will resent the hell out of it.

WRITE

Annie Dillard said
to close the blinds.

Marc Chagall claimed:
*The presence of real objects
is a nightmare for me.*

Stephen King tells us
to strip the *television's
electric plug-wire, wrap
a spike around it, and then
stick it back into the wall.
See what blows, and how far.*

And so it is that we write
at a table on a blank wall
in a small shroud of light,
surrounded by darkness.

GLUT

This poem arrived
at the back door
of my stingy mind
with too many words
in its pitiful hands.

And I allowed it in,
but made quite clear,
I would only have time
to write its last few lines.

Which turn out to be:

> too many words,
> too many lines,
> too many poems.

THERAPY

Take away
my guilt, shame,
the pain they've caused,

as well as the collection
I so meticulously curate
of all the little tableaus
I've glued together
in their honor,

and what's left
that would be
of any interest
to a reader?

Abundance

When will
these arms and legs,

these fingers that hold
the pen, or the pen
itself for that matter,

along with each new day
I'm allowed to use them,

be miracle enough?

BONE

know your own bone.

~ Henry David Thoreau

I've read the words
before and after these.

He meant well. Yet,
much as I loved my walk
around Walden Pond
during a time of great
gnawing on my own,

I believe he should've gone
deeper into the woods
of Massachusetts
to bury his.

WONKA

It's always some
Parnassian nut-job
who lives in a great
kaleidoscopic pyramid
out on the edge of town,

some psychedelic dill-weed
selling gastronomic delusions
of chocolate-covered bunnies
and foil-wrapped garden gnomes
pulled from piñon-encrusted
top hats made of toffee.

ENDS

Among granite
and bent red cedar,
not far from a coast,

he built an empire
to house his plans
for the cause of art.

And it was…
    he believed…
        about the art,

until the empire
did what empires
are designed to do.

GOING COLD

She reads her tall poems,
all four feet and three inches
of her, as if she were the ghost
of Marlon Brando come back
with laryngitis, barely audible,
teeth tight together, words
slipping through one half
of a colorless upper lip
in order to preserve
what precious little
body heat
is left.

EXPOSITION

Apparently she saw
a tad too much
of herself

in a short poem
I'd written about
another woman.

Still…
truth aside…

I received a colorful,
but mostly purple,
dreadful earful.

HMMM...

A tattered school picture
of my daughter, maybe
third or fourth grade,

marks my daily place
in the pages of Bukowski's
Mockingbird Wish Me Luck.

And the appropriateness
of this, or not, concerns me
more than you might think.

ABSTRACTION

I stood, as a beholder
in the eye of high art,
before the dead horse
on the floor with a sign
sticking out of its side
in the Tate Modern,

and began to wonder
where it is a good soldier
might get a decent margarita
on the god-forsaken streets
of Bankside, London.

EULOGY FOR A BASTARD

We gather here today,
   under a dark sky
   and certain sense
   of disorientation,

to scratch our heads
and armpits as one of us
offers a careful rendering
of disingenuous words
over one of God's
few regrets.

SIMILE

Typed or written out
it always makes me smile,
this jester of the word-world.
(Which is a metaphor. I know.)

But "simile" in print is so much
like "smile," I can hardly ever
help myself. Often having to
read the sentence twice
to make sure
I got it
right.

COMPARISON

In the hands of a master,
   once it is done,
      the original—
         the thing itself—

can never be remembered
without the specter
of its likeness.

PROBABILITY

The quiet street on which
I gave up my only virginity
contains the word *wood*
within the compound
structure of its name.

And I'm wondering,
being the academic I am,
if anyone has looked into
the statistical likelihood
of such a thing.

WEIGHTITUDE

Let this be
the *first known use*
of a great new word.

Take note, o etymologists
with nothing better to do.

I   have said it first.
And yes, I do feel
the full gravidity
of this moment.

Epiphanic

To step away
from prose
is an act of will.
A point of language
from which we never
return. Like leaving
the church of the way
we've always done things.

CARPE

Ok.
So it doesn't mean
to "seize,"
but to "pick"
or "pluck."

Does that change
what you would do
with this good day?

Especially if one of its
other verbal variations
is to: "pluck off"?

MULTITASKING

A shoddy word
hammered together
with corroded nails
in the musty workshop
of a stoned, unlicensed
subcontractor.

The prefix and root
sharing no flat edge.
The nonfinite suffix
letting us know
the job
will never
be done.

ZYMURGY

Scientists needed
not a big word, but one
no one could pronounce,

to name the questionable
"branch of chemistry"
dreamed up by bored
fraternity brothers
with hangovers.

A word bound
to be the last entry
in most dictionaries.

ARS POETICA:
POEMS AND THEIR PROBLEMS

This being the first
   and the worst
      of their many:

   Poems about poems,
   poets, and poetry.

A sad set of tracks
we try to cover
by giving them
Latinate titles.

and furthermore...

< O >

I never knew what you all wanted,
so I gave you everything.

~ Bruce Cockburn

MOONWALK

Much, much moon
on my walk tonight.
A madness almost
to its lumination.

Not a meanness,
mind you. But a
buxom and full-tilt
lunatic moonness.

LESS

Less lives down
at the quiet end
of degrees, usually
hoping for a low-key
night at home

with whatever
is left over
in the fridge

and a bottle,
already open,
that needs to be
finished off.

MORE

More runs hot,
spewing smoke and ash.

Always on the make
for a good stiff drink,
a quick lay, and
an even faster buck.

While crystal eyes
and a better heart
cry... softly...
in their bed
all night.

WATER – I

As God's great sun
and our golf courses,
along with The Venetian
in Las Vegas, continue
to suck the table dry,

we stand, still smiling,
yet a little concerned,
on receding shorelines

like passengers on the bow
of the RMS Titanic, waving
to their loved ones lining
the Port of Southampton.

WATER – II

A thing, like love,
we cannot live without,

which, at the same time,
kills us slowly because

of the tainted things
that seep into
its supply.

MANNA

… for Vedran Smailovic

God is stingier
than we give him credit for.

He can't just throw the stuff
around. We'd take it for granted,

like Israelites. But on rare occasions,
we hear it falling, as in the gut strings

and bow of "The Cellist of Sarajevo"
playing Albinoni's *Adagio in G Minor*

in the rubble and burned out ruin
of the National Library, bullets

and bombs the only choir
singing in the broken air

of the shattered stage
behind him.

PAIRS

Near her school yesterday,
it was not my daughter
but two other daughters
of four other parents
who died by the hands—

    yet another distracted pair
    of hands not on their wheel.
    A pair that lived to not be
    on the wheel again someday—

hands attached to their two arms,
making two sets of limbs and digits
that worked together to pull down
a pair of eyes—eyes that upraised

    could have saved
    a pair of girls.

FORGIVENESS

is like
a freshly fallen
coconut.

There is milk,
even meat,
inside.

But getting to it
is the damnedest thing.

114

INDEPENDENCE

No use
continuing
to declare it.

When the computers
all crash,
we'll go down
with them.

ANGER

Anger, like any
good American,
consumes more
than it needs
to survive,

more psychic calories
than its meager allotment
of joules can burn through
in any given moment
of ill-aimed energy.

PRAYER

Prayer,
like writing poetry,
cannot be taught.

A gift so sacred
its Muse could not
    be named.

A talent for hope
that I've never held.

A tool quite deadly
for the devil himself
in the hands and heart
of my anxious mother.

CHURCH

To step over
that pious threshold
and set out into the world—
    wandering its wildnesses
    for not quite forty years—

then one day stumble upon
the long lost garden where
the God of all creation
maintains a modest hut,
his tools strewn all about,

makes going back to a building
he only visits now and then
feel like forfeiture.

DISORDER

A marker doled out
by those who believe
they have not the same
        or some other.

A condition we give
some compound name
from one of the 943 pages
in the *DSM-IV Manual
        of Mental Disorders.*

Diagnoses for those who
clearly have something
        or some other.

Designations to calm us,
as we avoid the hard light
of God's more creative
        disruptions.

ANTISTHENES

> We tried cynicism; some of us
> succeeded.
>
> ~ Adam Zagajewski

Cynics are not
pessimists.

They just prefer
to shrewdly minimalize
their optimism.

ADAPTATION

Victoriana,
    a tiny plant

that requires almost
nothing: only air

and some amount
of light: the reason

we will die off
first.

COUNTERFEITER

The intelligent,
less greedy felon

reproduces flawless
one dollar bills

and takes his time.

HONEST

Think of the answer
you would never give
to the question: *So,
how's it going?*

That
is what
I want to know
about you.

Renovation

First,
buy a nice
DuraGuard®
Antimicrobial
toilet seat

made of 100%
recycled molded wood
with the high-gloss finish
and non-tarnish hinges.

Next, install that sucker.

Then, sit for a spell
while you figure out
what to do next.

LEAFBLOWER

O plastic orange
    piece of crap
designed by shits
    to burn fossil crap
for no shitful purpose
    other than to blow
our lawn-crap
    from one side
of our shitty sidewalks
    to the crappy other.

Cheers

We toast
the big things
with champagne
or whatever's close
because the thing
is finally over, or
it's about to begin,
and now we sort of
feel nervous because
we don't, to be honest,
like change.

BORING

> They are so boring you get tired of
> them even when they're not around.
>
> ~ William Stafford's mother

Boring to the point that a certain
ontological fascination sets in,
and we begin to wonder
        what absences
must've been present
for such a shocking
level and degree
of boringness
to develop.

WORRY

is one of those things
we often do to death.

When my mother says
she is "a little worried,"
she is lying. As are most

mothers. For if not to death,
we are at least worried sick.
And we love, if not live for,
this sickness and death.

How else could
the 5 O'clock News
survive?

AXIAL

My tires spin
over roads wrapped
around the ball of earth
that orbits a rotating sun
wheeling its elliptical way
in the centrifugal arms of
a galaxy that whirls and
wobbles around some
dark unknowable
that is the un-
doing

of a circle.

ASKANCE

A grown man
sticks his philosophy
    somewhat askew
to his pickup's bumper,

off-road tires peeling out
in the stoplight's shifting
from red back to green,

the hot rubber screaming
his absolute unwillingness
to pause and discuss

the finer points
of our apparent
disagreement.

RECRUIT

... on Memorial Day

He got the haircut
and donned the uniform
because "almost dying"
would be a cool thing
to be able to claim
when he got back
to the States.

The "actually dying,"

he had not
signed up for.

SOUND EFFECTS

Look. We, the old—
    according to you,
        the young—

do not hate noise
because we are old—
    according to you—

but because we
tried it once too—

used it, like you are now,
to ward off the silence
and its terrifying secrets—

and found, in the end,
that it doesn't work.

CARPE ANNUM

Time is a bitch—
    no slight to the sweet, furry
    little head of our household.

But between the interminable
length of it that stretches out
the hot-summer years of youth

and the unnerving lack of it
that plagues the later decades
of sore feet and incontinence,

we may only have… say…
one good year somewhere
in our mid 30s. Though…

I don't remember mine.

BURGEON

The world is still
too much with us,
dear Wordsworth.
Both late and soon.

Only now—
by way of cell phones,
YouTube, and stone-
cutting bandsaws—

it has hit upon
more effective
means.

PROVENANCE

All through the night
and into a gray morning,
dark walls of rain have fallen
on this drought-stricken plain.

But it's late in the spring of '13
and the planet's affair with ice.

So, by the end of the summer
we'll be back to short-winded
prognostications over
the certain cause
of the Third
World War.

EN MEXICO

Where things are made.

Though not as many
as are made
in China.

Things
that come cheap.

Though only to those
who buy them.

AH, PARIS

There is
romance
in the air.

Only… a dry
and strange lack
of enthusiasm for it

on the part of
the Parisians
themselves.

FLÂNEUR

Some mornings say,

I think we'll walk
wherever we go today.
Maybe find a giant garden.
Spend inordinate hours there.

Yes, some mornings are just
a bit more French than others,

suggesting things on that walk
like, *I think maybe next year*
we should go ahead and push
for a 20-hour work week.

THE HUM

Taos adds
a bright shade
of blood-red
to the cheeks
of those who
move here from
Texas and California.

A shade that often
turns to black
and dark blue
for those who
stay too long.

ELEMENTS

Fire, or wind,
or a wave the size
of a small mountain

comes along to gut
and clean the insides
of all we thought
we had to have
to live in this world,

releasing us from
its corporeal weight,
yet tying us forever
to the burden
of its memory.

TORNADO

It has a thing for May
and trailer parks.

That dark anger
that begins to twist

then spin when warm air
rises off the roasting flesh

of a planet slowly
turning on the spit

of its dried up
patience.

DROUGHT

They say it will take
years for Lake Travis
to stop being merely
the Colorado River again

    ...the river time
      and erosion
      intended...

before it fills back up
with our original sense
of engineering and purpose,

    ...which is,
      of course...

Sea Doos and Baja 38 Special
Twin Mercury 502 MAG
power boats.

FATTENING

A big American flag
slithers and whips
in front of bright
white clouds behind
Austin's Capitol dome.

Red snakes snapping
in the crisp, ever-changing
wind growling in the gut
of a young nation
that swallowed
capitalism
whole.

CLEANSING

June, and there's ice
in the Texas Panhandle.

Crack a joke about global
warming, if you must.

But know that Mother Earth
has stirred after a lengthy nap,
rubbed her blue eyes in disbelief,

and grabbed the big broom over by
the ShopVac, 'cause she's pissed
at the way we've left the place.

TESTAMENT

I drove right through the devil
on U.S. 84 in Clovis, New Mexico.

Twisting wind wrenched the car
as he danced his gritty little jig.

And when the dust cleared away,
back to merely scorching desolation,

a billboard posting a loose translation
of Moses' Ten Commandments

roared right through the glare
of my bug-smeared windshield.

DISPENSATION

Corrugated messages
from a bored God rattle
in the rush and the whip
of passing tractor-trailers
on West Texas two-lanes
tessellated with windmills
and tangles of pear cactus

like rusty tin prophets
whose alarm cries fall
on the deaf eyes
of mile-weary
travelers.

SPRING

As the Bradford Pear
bursts into Easter-white
blossoms, the hoary oak
clings to its last three
brittle brown leaves—
aquiline fingers shaking
a curled up disapproval
of the zealous pear's
garish disregard
for the likelihood
of a late freeze.

More Than

> Poetry is joy hiding despair.
>
> ~ Adam Zagajewski

I suppose
living in the time
just before the earth

runs out of potable water,
catches fire, and purges
the human population,

is better than living
in the during, or
the just after.

Less Than

He stands on top of a picnic table
outside the Tantra Coffeehouse

with nothing on but gym shorts
and a Twain-shock of white hair.

Maybe 65, but packing the pects
and biceps of a 20-something

welterweight. His hands raised
to God and oncoming traffic

in praise of his immaculate
tan and tight six-pack. Flexing

right in the face of my shame
over this morning's pastry.

AND FURTHERMORE …

< O >

MORE THAN MORE

Less is
not as much,
never a big deal
and hardly ever
what we want.

Which mystifies us
every time a prophet
or philosopher sings
that it just might be,
at the proverbial end
of the proverbial day,

    everything.

løss is more bio:

Nathan Brown is a songwriter, photographer, and award-winning poet from Norman, Oklahoma. He more or less holds a PhD in *Creative and Professional Writing* from the university there and currently serves as the Poet Laureate for the state of Oklahoma (2013 – 2014).

For more information, or to order books and CDs, go to:

brownlines.com